T0378976

oasis
talking
shite

*Compiled and Edited by **Not** the **Gallagher Brothers***

Simon & Schuster
New York Amsterdam/Antwerp London
Toronto Sydney/Melbourne New Delhi

Liam: You've got to talk a lot of shit to get to the nitty-gritty truth. The more shit you say, the more you get to the absolute point.

Noel: Writing songs is difficult; talking shit is easy. In fact, that is going to be the name of my audiobook: *Talking Shit Is Easy.*

Liam: I give a fuck *not* to give a fuck, d'you know what I mean?

Liam: It's just me and me brother having arguments in a band. If we weren't in a band, we'd be havin' it in the house. If we had a greengrocers, Gallaghers' Greengrocers, we'd argue over which way we set out the apples or the fuckin' pears.

Noel: [Liam's] fans come up to him after shows and I hear him giving all this gobshite, and I think, "Shut up, you twat, I babysat for you."

Noel: Hard work and a fucking filthy tongue, that's what I inherited from my mum. She taught the nineties how to swear.

Liam: I know a lot of people have fucking dickheads as mams, but my mam's cool as fuck, absolute cool as fuck. Everything that is good about me is definitely from her.

Q: What is the worst thing anyone's said to you?

Liam: "Are you Noel Gallagher?"

———

Q: What's the worst psychological torture you can imagine suffering?

Noel: Being sat beside Liam on a fifteen-hour flight.

Noel: You can't predict anything with my band. . . . I can actually envision a day you'll be over the Indian Ocean and an air stewardess will come back and say, "Mr. Gallagher? Your brother has fallen out of the plane." I'd be like, "Where's he landed? Is it shark-infested? Great!"

Liam: I did fall out of a helicopter, but it was on the ground.

Noel: Every ludicrous thing I've ever said, I accepted the consequences, because I don't think I've ever said, "Oh, it was taken out of context, that." Fucking wankers say that.

Guess the Wanker, Part I

A. Ol' dinosaur hips . . . poor sod, he's got to dance until he's 108.

B. Sweaty old mushroom.

C. A cabbage.

D: That geezer with the two pieces of lettuce stuck on the side of his head.

E. Anyone who has four haircuts on the same head has got to be respected.

1

4

2

5

3

Liam: **Oasis was definitely like a fucking Ferrari: great to look at, great to drive. It would spin out of control every now and again when you go too fast.**

Noel: I'd literally done all the drugs that I'd had. There was none left in London. I'd done them all. And I was like, "Right, well, that fucking was interesting. Okay, well, I've done that now. Can we buy me a bike?"

Liam: You mean which is still my favourite nostril? Are we talking power nostril here? The left, definitely the left. The right's the super sub. The left starts the match, does the full ninety minutes, then the right comes in for extra time and penalties!

Q: Would you shave your eyebrows?
Noel: I shave them every morning, and this is where they are at seven o'clock at night. They're like little caterpillars.

———

Q: What's Noel's best quality?
Liam: He's got lovely, lovely eyebrows.

Liam: Have you seen the size of it? That head is like the changing of the guards, like a bearskin. [Noel's] got one of them on his little body!

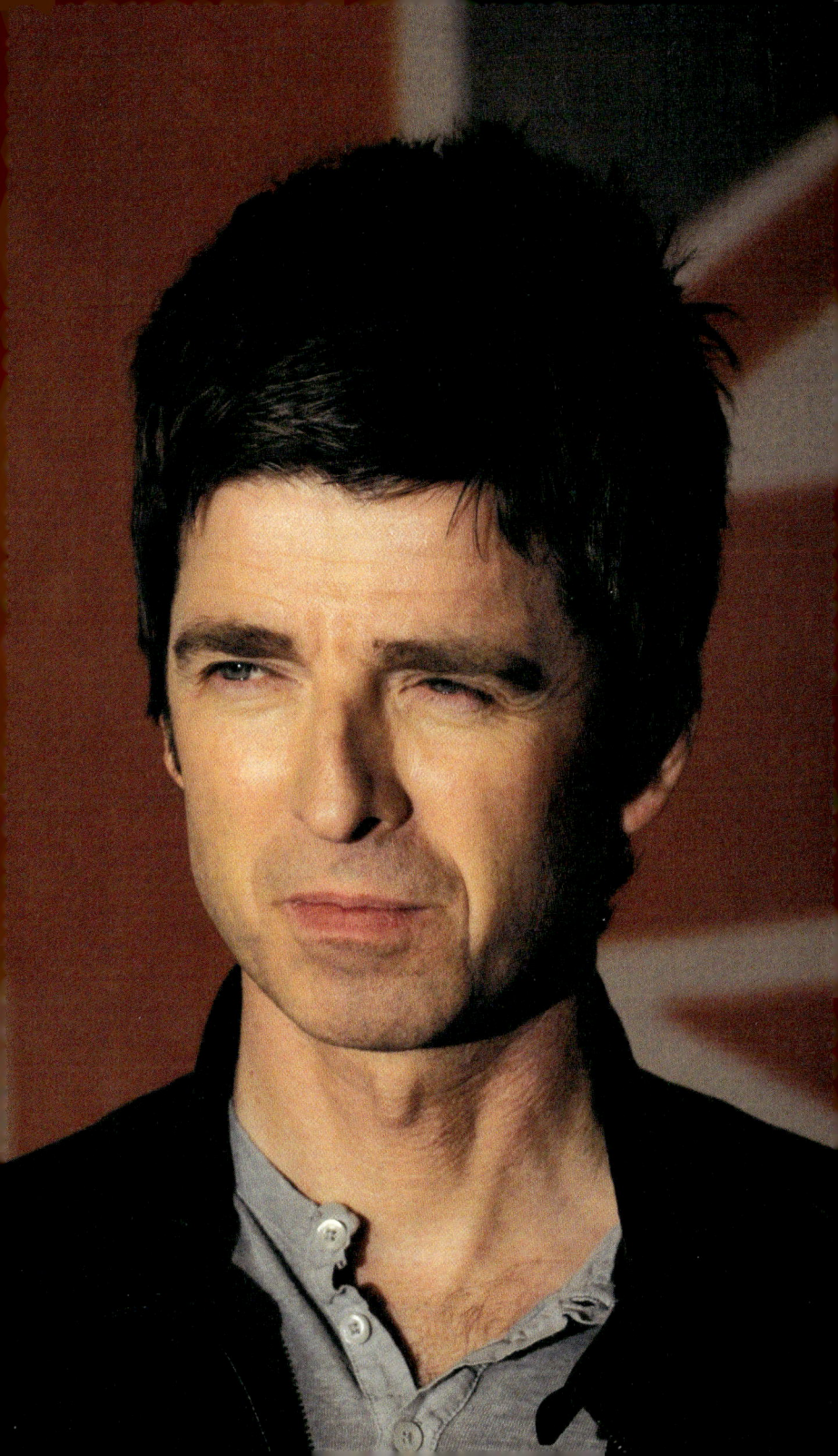

Liam: If I lost my hair you would never see me on that stage again. 'Cos there's no place for baldness in rock 'n' roll.

———

Noel: The thing about Liam and his hairdos is when he gets a new one, you think, "That looks absolutely rubbish," then six weeks later everyone on Oxford Street has got one.

Noel: Liam lives in Disneyland, y'know what I mean? He's started to carry a man bag, which is very disturbing.

Noel: George Harrison was always the silent Beatle. Personally, I think he should keep that image up.

—

Liam: I know for a fact that I'd never, ever feel the need to have a ruck or a brawl with McCartney. He's not even worth it.

—

Noel: The only reason people revere John Lennon is because he's not around to be shit.

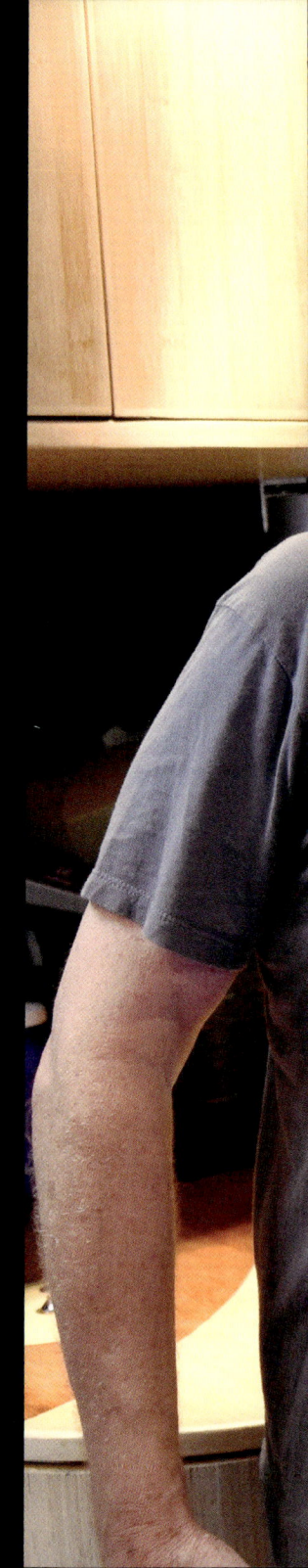

Liam: Ringo's a dude, man.

Liam: Sit on me knee.

Noel: You're the puppet. You sit on my fucking knee.

Noel: What I was bad at was spelling. Still am. Anything over six letters and that's me gone.

Noel: Flip-flops and the word "latte" make me uncomfortable. (2006)

———

Noel: I hate that word, "toddy." It makes me feel uncomfortable, that and the word "latte." (2009)

———

Noel: "Latte" is one of the shittiest words in all of language. (2017)

Liam: I find words really hard.

Noel: What really fucking annoys me about books is when you go to the bookshop and you'll see a book—the book will be titled *The Happiness of the Homosexual Squirrel*—and I'll say, "What's that book about?" They'll say, "Oh, it's about drug addicts." So what the fucking hell's that title, then? You know, "*How to Catch a Hippo*, what's that about?" "Oh, it's about one woman's fucking erotic journey across fucking Eastern Europe." People who write books are fucking idiots.

Liam: Books are for losers. I never need to live others' stories; mine is enough. Those who read books haven't imagination. They're not able to read their own mind, their own thoughts. Mine are really enough.

Liam: My favourite book is *The Lion, the Witch and the Wardrobe*. I like it. I like that thing of just going in a wardrobe.

Liam: I didn't join a band to be pushed about by some twat with a camera. . . . I'll [slap 'em] until they drag me into my grave. I'll be slapping 'em when they're taking pictures of my tomb, man.

Q: Has Liam really got a photographic memory as he once boasted?

Liam: Absolutely. Totally.

Q: Really?

Liam: What is a photographic memory?

Guess the Wanker, Part II

A. He looks like Zorro on doughnuts.

B. I just don't see what all the fuss is about. I don't like her music. I think it's music for fucking grannies.

C. That fucking slack-jawed fuckwit.

D. Do you ever look at the sky and think, "I'm glad I'm alive"? After I heard ____, I thought, "I'm actually alive to hear the shittiest band of all time. . . . Of all the bands that have gone before and all the bands that'll be in the future, I was around when the worst was around."

E. My eleven-year-old daughter's bang into her, but it's not for me, is it? A bird dressed in a suit made of meat? I'm forty-four—I'm not supposed to get that.

1

2

3

4

5

Noel: [Liam's] like a squeaky toy that swears a lot . . . in a blazer.

Liam: Jazz is fucking shit. Jazz is fucking stupid.

Liam: The big-bang theory? Not really a theory, is it? What, one explosion and that was it? Bit fucking boring, if you ask me.

Q: Are you scared of dying?

Liam: No, because I've already done it before. Done it a couple of times and it's a piece of piss. There is nothing to it—you just sit there and wait for it to happen. Big deal.

Noel: I'm not really bothered 'cos I won't be [at my funeral]. I don't give a shit.

Liam: I won't be getting buried, anyway. I'm going to be mummified and put on display in a museum.

Noel: I don't believe that on a Monday morning some white-bearded geezer with fuckin' nothing better to do created the planets. Bollocks to that!

Liam: I won't change—not unless the geezer with the big beard lands down in front of me and pulls a giraffe out of his nostril and goes, "I'm God—you've got to be like this, you've got to be like that." But until that happens, then they can fuck right off.

Liam: If I was God, which I'm not, which maybe I might be, but I'm not saying I'm not, so there. . . . If I had a big house in the sky and a load of sheep turning up to lick my feet, I'd tell 'em to fuck right off.

Noel: If I ever get to go to the moon, I'll probably just stand on the moon and go, "Oh yeah, alright, fair enough, can I go home now?" (1995)

Noel: I'd give up everything I fucking ever made out of this band to go to another planet with some aliens. I'd give all I've got to go to the moon. (2005)

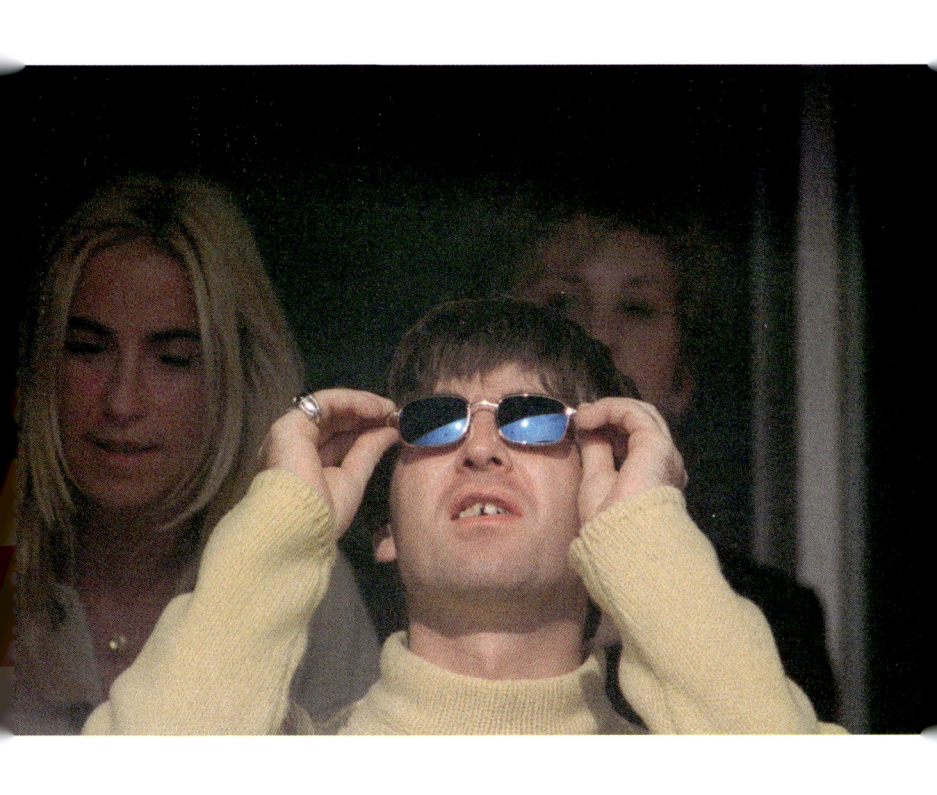

Liam: I'd do their fuckin' heads in, them aliens, man. Freak 'em right out. They'd be like, "Farking hell, farking hell! Let's get back to Planet Knob!" I'd do their heads in, me, frighten the life out of them! That's why they haven't landed yet. They're going, "Fuck that, can't land while he's about!" I'd take them out and get them fucking slaughtered. I would make them turn green then!

Noel: Fuck trees, man. . . . Dogs piss on them.

Liam: Fuck the sea. I ain't going in that. Fuck that, mate. That ain't meant for us. That's meant for the sharks, and the jellyfish, tadpoles, and stuff. But a hot tub? I'm alright in a hot tub. Can hang about in there for a bit.

Noel: See, I like pirates. That'd be a good occupation, wouldn't it? I'd like to have been a pirate, if I wasn't a rock star. Some might say pirates are earlier-day rock stars. Of course, on the sea.

Noel: Liam, clearly, would have liked to have had my talent as a songwriter, and there is not a day goes by where I don't wish I could rock a parka like that man.

Q: Have you ever done yoga?

Liam: I've done it once and I got stuck.

Noel: Who gives a fuck about sport, all that bollocks, running around in shorts and that! Fuck that nonsense!

Liam: Rock stars exercising? I don't think it's right. You either got it or you ain't.

Noel: Skateboarding's for fucking little idiots. Skateboarders can, quite frankly, go fuck themselves. I've never seen a skateboarder ever, in the streets, in the entire world, try and do something and not fall off.

Liam: Ten things I hate? Man United . . . just Man United. I just hate Man United. I hate Man United ten times.

Noel: I hate [Manchester United] and cannot stand them, their ground, or their manager. It's a hatred that steadily grows. I hate them more than yesterday.

Liam: Wayne Rooney looks like a fucking balloon with Weetabix crushed on top.

Liam: I fucking hate sleeping, me. Boring! I wish I didn't have to sleep—it's such a waste of time. I'd rather be up, living.

Liam: I'm getting up earlier and earlier now, man. I try and beat the alarm clock. The alarm goes off at six, and I try to get up at 5:59 just to do its head in.

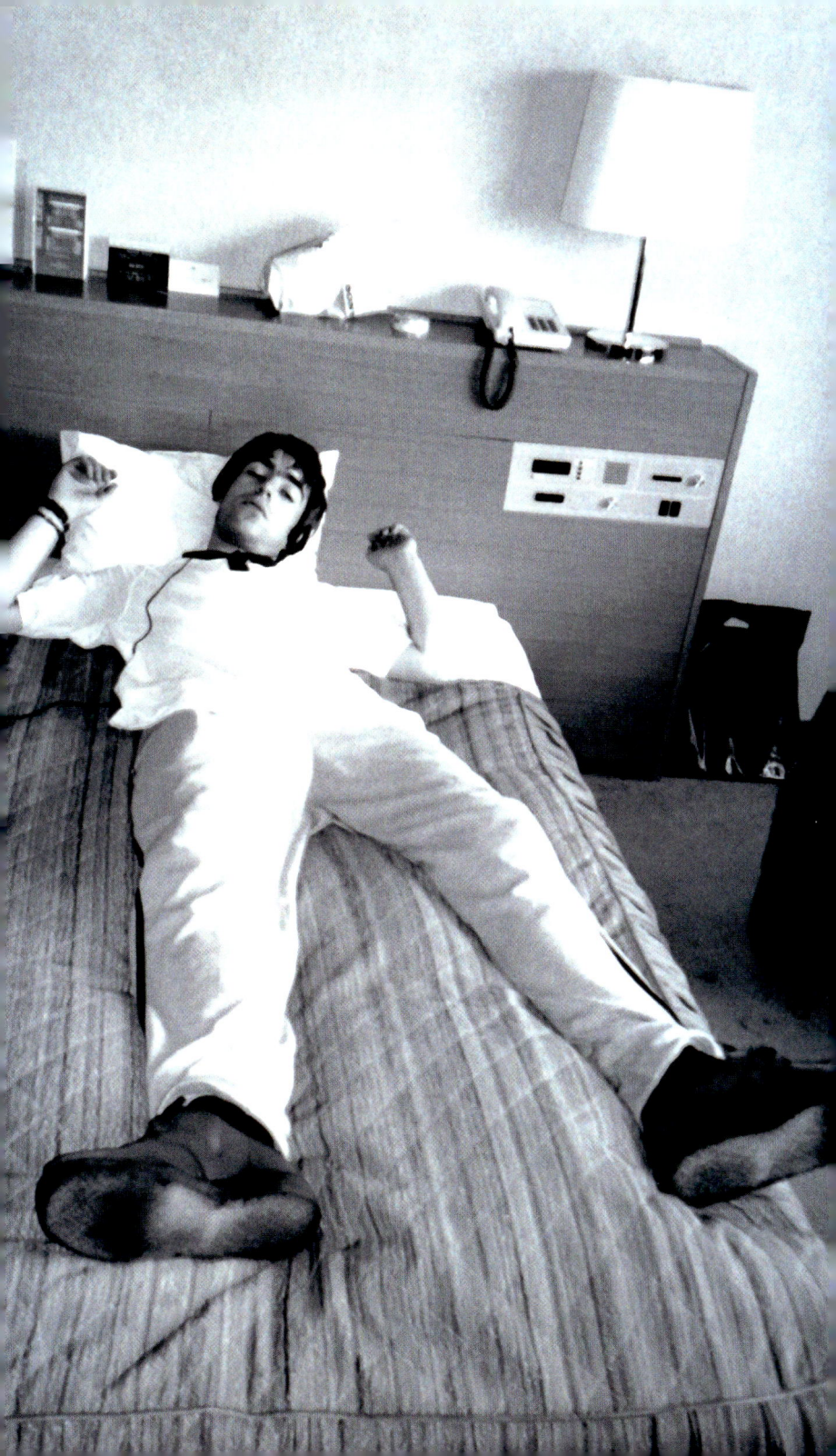

Noel: There's no reason, ever, to be late. Or early.

Noel: [My voice is] half a Guinness on a Tuesday. Liam's is ten shots of tequila on a fucking Friday night.

Liam: That's a problem with this fucking country, right here, right now. Too many fucking programmes on food, man. And then there's nothing on music. . . . You got loads of dicks baking fucking cakes and fucking bread and all that. Fuck off.

Q: What's your favourite biscuit?

Noel: It's got to be the chocolate digestive, plain or milk. Unsurpassable in the biscuit world.

———

Liam: I'll tell you another top biscuit: Garibaldis. They are boring as fuck but mega.

Guess the Wanker, Part III

A. They look like fucking Amish people. You know, them ones with the big sideys that don't use electricity? Growing their own food and putting barns up?

B. It's just music for hairdressers, isn't it?

C. I have never seen a ____ fan. I have never seen anyone with a ____ shirt or been around someone's house that has a fucking ____ record. Where do their fans fucking come from? Where are they? I reckon they buy them.

D. Fuck *Blade Runner. Blade Runner* is _____. *Star Wars* is Oasis.

E. Looks like a geography teacher.

1

4

2

5

3

Liam: Doing duets is for girls.

———

Liam: I'm down with my feminine side, without a fucking doubt.

Liam: You never see me down film premieres even though I get invited to about a hundred a week. I hate standing there with all those knobs coming in in dresses they've borrowed. Fuck off!

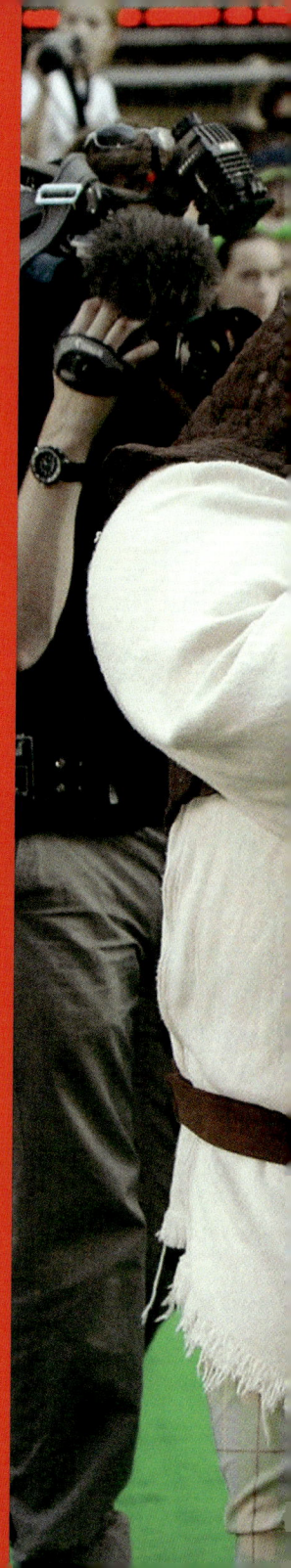

Noel: I'd also do a private party at Jabba's palace if the bitcoinage was right.

Noel: My fragrance? Oh, it's coming, it's coming. Toe-Rag, it's going to be called. And the bottle's going to be a massive toe.

Noel: My record company just bought me a £60,000 Rolls for Christmas. But I can't drive. I just get in the back and laugh my arse off.

Noel: I hate the way anyone from the working class who makes money, the working class turns on them. The people in my band, we'll be working class till we die. We were brought up socialists and we'll die socialists.

Liam: Doesn't matter who you fucking vote for. It'll still be shit unless you join a band.

Noel: Legalize drugs. Kill all the people who like grunge music. Kill all surfboarders. Melt the snow. Anybody who wears a cowboy hat should get the electric chair. Generally have a good time. With that platform, I think I can get you elected. I think I can get myself elected.

Liam: [The royal family] are always going to be here, just like . . . the lampposts.

Noel: The funniest thing was that the queen's got her own bog at Number Ten, and I've had a shit in it. . . . Only me and the queen have ever shat in that bog, ever. Which is great, innit? A big Gallagher turd next to a royal one, floating through the U-bend.

Liam: I want people to know when I've farted, do you know what I mean? . . . Because you're proud of it, aren't you? When it's silent and that, sometimes they take credit for it. But you want it to just tear the house down, don't you?

Liam: I didn't have a guitar habit because I could never play; I had a tambourine habit once, though. But, to be honest, you play one tambourine, you've played them all, mate.

Noel: [Liam's] the man who put the "tit" in attitude.

Noel: Americans just fundamentally do not get it. That is the one thing about Yanks, right? They. Do. Not. Get. It. Whatever it is, they don't fucking get it.

———

Liam: Didn't really get on with LA. I found it a bit weird. It was either mental and dark and full of heroin, or it was full of fucking rye bread and sparkling water.

———

Noel: It's just that America is a really delicate flower that needs a lot of attention, and we're not those kind of people.

Liam: SpongeBob is a fucking mental, full-of-beans, enthusiastic sponge that lives at the bottom of the sea in Bikini Bottom. He's mad for it. He's got a mate called Squidward who plays the clarinet and is grumpy like our kid Noel.

———

Noel: There's one on the Cartoon Network called *SpongeBug SquarePants*! It's this little sponge bug and he's got chocolate square shorts and he lives at the bottom of the sea, and it's about his adventures. Fucking mega!

Noel: [Liam's] always going on to me about his song "The Meaning of Soul." I said, "I've seen the meaning of soul. If you holding SpongeBob SquarePants's hand in a magazine isn't the meaning of fucking soul, I don't know what is."

Liam: No one knows where your soul goes. What is a soul? You've got a voice, a big dick, or a fucking top pair of trainers. What's a soul?

Liam: The main thing we're talking about here is this: any dick who wants it, regardless of what time or day or what shoes I've got on . . . anyone who wants a rumble will get it. . . . And there'll be no big chaps around, man. Just me and me dick, man. And I'll hit him with me knob.

Noel: I can't get my head round pop music [right now]. It all sounds the same. It's all on the same frequency. It all seems designed to aggravate my teeth.

Guess the Wanker, Part IV

A. Listen, the only reason ____ do a fookin' video in fookin' black and white is because they look like a bunch of spotty little idiots in color.

B. She's quite unnecessary.

C. I'm not having anyone with ginger hair making music. I can't go down that road. I'm sure she's a nice girl, but she sounds like someone has stood on her fucking foot.

D. [He] sounds like an artist from the Renaissance period.

E. If you could get slapped on the NHS, if they could provide it as a medical service, then I think he'd definitely need to be taken to hospital and held down by some people in white coats and just slapped about the face for half an hour.

1

2

4

3

5

Noel: Fuck art. Drawing pictures—big deal.

Noel: Well, I hate Christmas, and you can quote me on that. I hate the silly music they play on the radio, I hate the adverts on the telly, I don't like mince pies, and I hate turkey. I can't be arsed getting involved. I was on the verge of saying to my daughter, "There is no Father Christmas." I'm looking forward to breaking the news in about two years' time.

Liam: I'm in the top two human beings on the planet.

Q: Who else is there?

Liam: I dunno. Could be Elvis. Could be Gandhi. Could be the street sweeper. Could be you.

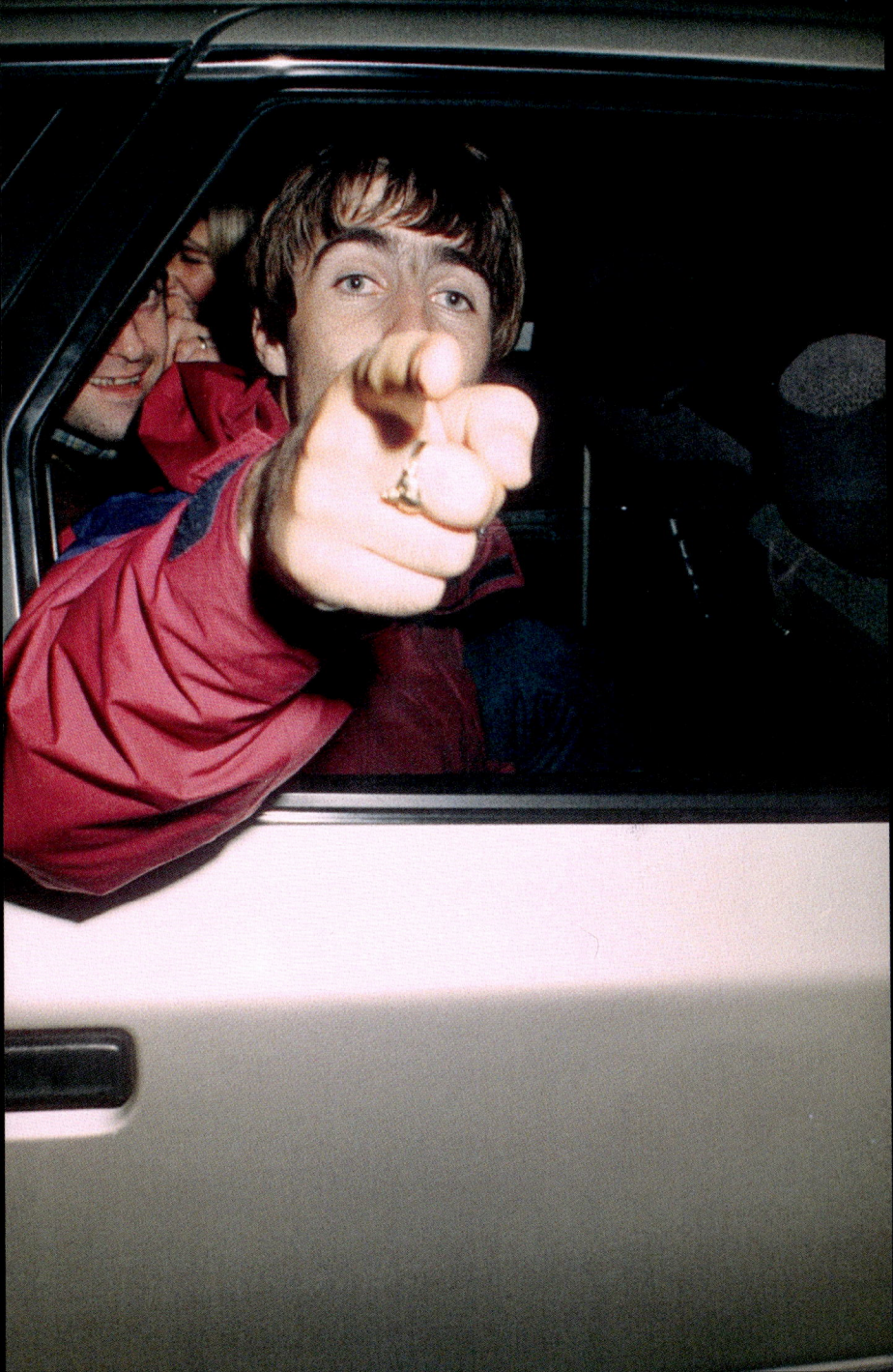

Liam: I could have multiple personalities, but they are all fucking amazing. Whoever they are, they are all fucking great.

Noel: [Liam's] not as good as John Lennon. He's not even as good as Jack Lemmon.

Liam: I am a top dad, without a doubt. I've seen other dads at school and they haven't got a fooking clue, they talk to their kids like idiots. I'm cool, man.

Liam: [My kids] also like that bloke, WhatsApp Ricky. You know, the American geezer, stylish, funny gold teeth . . .

Q: You mean A$AP Rocky?

Liam: Oh, yeah, that's the fella. WhatsApp Ricky—that's a better fucking name anyway.

Noel: The internet is shite. . . . You can't get *Match of the Day* on it, you know what I mean? Or porno movies, or anything. . . . It's just a lot of writing, innit? (1997)

Noel: I have to admit I thought [the internet] was going to be a fad which was going to pass in about six months, but you know . . . (2000)

Noel: People sending you stupid videos of fucking goats singing Oasis songs that's been done by AI, and you just think . . . Actually, that sounds better than Liam. (2023)

Liam: No, I don't like [the internet], man. . . . I feel like a fuckin' ass with it, to tell you the truth. I don't like computers and it's probably because I can't use them, but I'm just not into it. I'm just an old fart.

Noel: I don't need to be on Facebook. I've got six friends. Trying to get rid of one of those so I can count them all on one hand, and that's me done, then.

Guess the Wanker, Part V

A. Boring as fuck. We called him Dermot Oblong.

B. The thing that gets me is, people will say that _____ [is] the Beatles and we're the Stones. The fact of the matter is, we're the Beatles *and* the Stones, and they're the fucking Monkees.

C. He looks like a dustbin man these days, but good luck to him.

D. It's music for posh brats.

E. It's fitting that he ended up as a cartoon. He always was a cartoon.

Key: A4. Liam on Damon Albarn; B2. Noel on Blur; C1. Noel on Damon Albarn; D3. Liam on Blur; E5. Noel on Damon Albarn

1

2

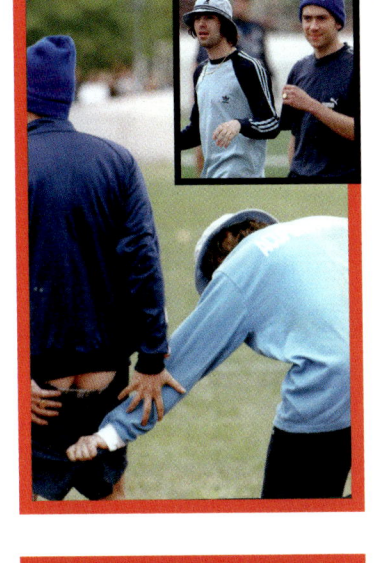

4

5

3

Q: Is there an American equivalent of Blur that you just can't stand?

Noel: Hole. Just say that word: "Hole."

Noel: I want to stop slagging other bands off, because I've met most of them and they're really nice people. But I have to be honest and say that they're not very good.

Guess the Wanker: Bonus Round

A. Stratford's finest Oasis tribute band.

B. It sounds like Blur.

1

2

Noel: I liked it better when we had to go and prove ourselves. I've only got to fookin' fart and it gets in the top 10 now.

Liam: I like Noel outside the band. Human Noel—that's my brother—I fucking adore him and I'd do anything for him. But the geezer that's in this fucking business, he's one of the biggest cocks in the universe.

—————

Noel: Liam knows that I love him; I don't have to tell him. I know that he loves me, and I really don't want to hear him telling me.

Noel: Would we get back together one day? As long as everybody is still alive and still has their hair, it's always a possibility.

Noel: Actually, I'm thinking of getting a contract drawn up which says, "If we ever split and get back together, I hereby give legal permission to anybody who wants to kick my fucking head in." They should make that standard when you sign a record deal, because there's nobody, absolutely nobody, who's better the second time around.

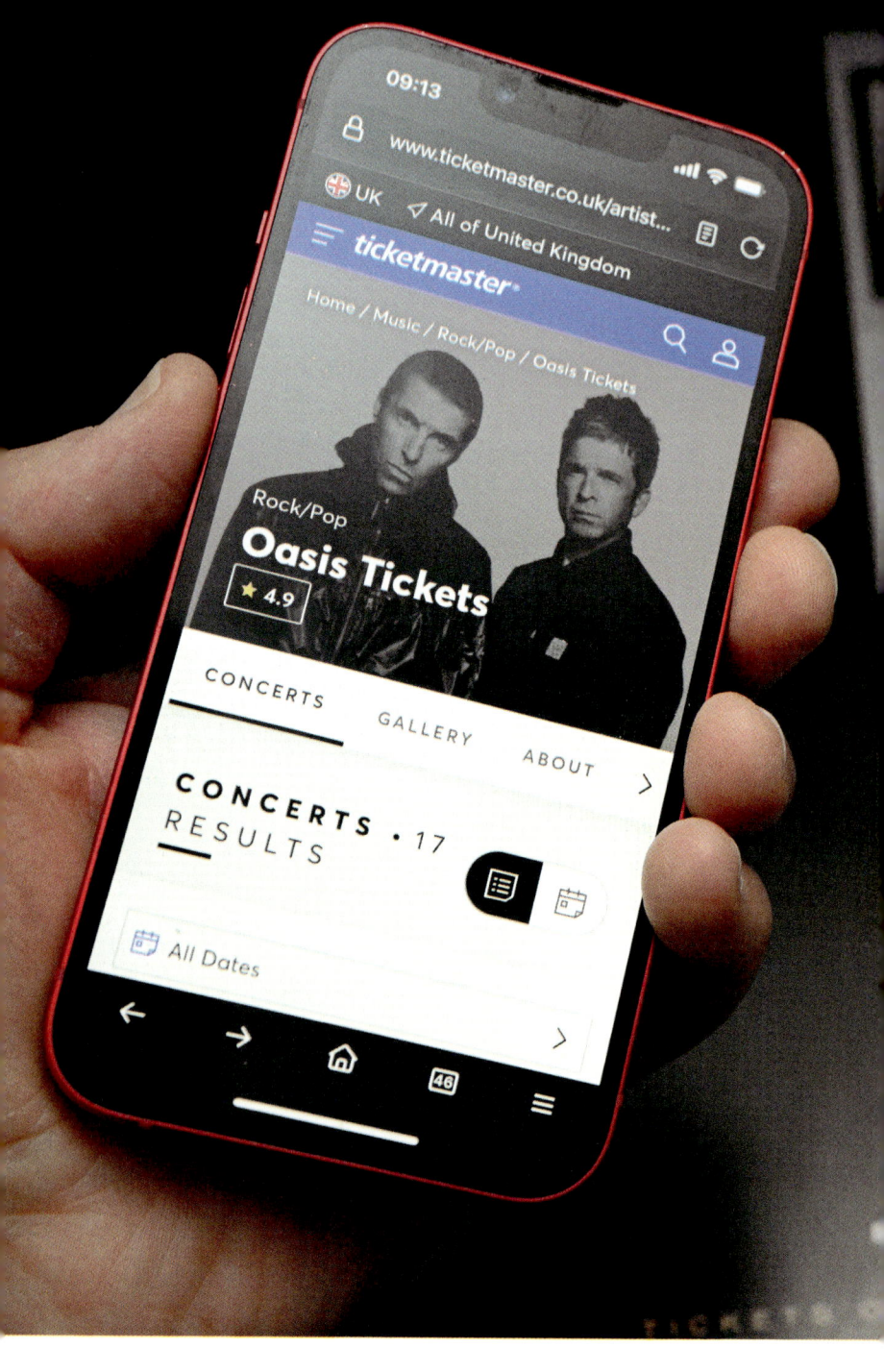

Liam: When rock 'n' roll calls, you've got to pick up the phone.

asis

ive '25

CARDIFF PRINCIPALITY STADIUM · 4TH / 5TH JULY
MANCHESTER HEATON PARK · 11TH / 12TH / 16TH / 19TH / 20TH JULY
LONDON WEMBLEY STADIUM · 25TH / 26TH JULY / 2ND / 3RD AUGUST
EDINBURGH SCOTTISH GAS MURRAYFIELD STADIUM · 8TH / 9TH / 12TH AUGUST
DUBLIN CROKE PARK · 16TH / 17TH AUGUST

SATURDAY

Text Credits: Many of the quotes herein were pulled from sources found on the website oasisinterviews.blogspot.com (OIB for short) and in the book *Mad for It: The Wit & Wisdom of the Gallaghers*, by archivist Paul Stokes, as well as the book *Supersonic: The Complete, Authorised and Uncut Interviews*, curated by Simon Halfon. When cited, the origin sources can be found in one of these places. Other specific sources are listed below. Text has been lightly edited for clarity. When redacted in the original source, curse words have been restored according to the authors' best Gallagherian discernment. **OIB:** p. 8 (*Rolling Stone*, May 18, 1995); p. 10 (*The Face*, August 1994); pp. 16 [bottom], 80 [bottom] (*Melody Maker*, December 1998); pp. 22b, 138, 156 (*GQ*, February 1998); p. 22c (*The Age*, November 25, 2005); p. 22d (*Uncut*, March 2000); p. 22e (*Q*, April 2000); pp. 34 [top], 60, 70, 116 [bottom] (*NME*, February 19, 2000); p. 38 (*The Age*, December 12, 2006); p. 40 [top] (*NY Rock*, December 1997); pp. 40 [middle], 76, 128 (*The Sunday Times*, February 18, 1996); p. 40 [bottom] (*GQ*, February 2000); pp. 44, 56, 66, 154 (*Select*, August 1997); pp. 46, 74, 130 (*Q*, February 1996); p. 48 [top] (*Elle*, 2006); pp. 54, 192 [bottom] (source unknown, 1997); p. 78 (*Daily Telegraph*, August 16, 1997); pp. 82, 108 [top] (*NME*, July 12, 1997); p. 84 (*Access*, November 1997); p. 96 (*NME*, June 24, 1995); p. 98 (*The Observer*, June 16, 2002); pp. 116 [top], 150 [bottom] (*NME*, February 26, 2000); p. 120 [top] (*Worldpop*, August 2000); pp. 134, 184 (*Rage*, September 1996); p. 148 [top] (*Select*, August 11, 1996); p. 152 (*The Observer*, June 19, 2005); p. 160a (*NME*, April 6, 2002); p. 160b, (Xfm, October 11, 2001); p. 160d (*Now*, May 2002); p. 164 (*Nuts*, January 21, 2005) p. 170 (*Worldpop*, January 2001); p. 176 [middle] (*Muse*, January 21, 2000); p. 178 (*Toronto Sun*, April 2000); p. 182a (*Uncut*, April 2004); p. 182c (*Melody Maker*, September 5, 1999); p. 182e (*Q*, May 2002); p. 190 (*The Guardian*, April 22, 1995) **Mad for It:** p. 18 [top] (48); p. 34 [bottom] (42); p. 72 [top] (107); p. 118b (86); p. 132 (61); p. 136 (68); p. 160c (88); p. 186 (85) **Supersonic:** p. 4 (303); p. 14 (76), p. 24 (xi), p. 90 (256); p. 148 [middle] (186); p. 168 (43) **Other sources:** p. 2 (*Esquire*, April 28, 2022); p. 6 (*The Guardian*, May 26, 2022); pp. 12, 20, 126 (*Esquire*, December 1, 2015); p. 16 [top] (*The Guardian*, October 17, 2017); p. 18 [bottom] (*NME*, February 18, 2022); pp. 22a, 68, 142, 174 (*GQ*, July 30, 2017); p. 26 (*Rolling Stone*, August 11, 2011); pp. 28, 58 (*Hot Press*, 2000); p. 30 [top] ("Noel Gallagher Webcast with Matt Morgan—22nd August 2011," posted August 22, 2011, by Noel Gallagher, YouTube); p. 30 [bottom] (*Vogue*, June 5, 2017); p. 32 (*The Telegraph*, September 14, 2019); p. 42 (*The Guardian*, February 19, 2018); p. 48 [middle] (Noel Gallagher, *Tales from the Middle of Nowhere*, 70, EPUB); p. 48 [bottom] (*iHeart*,

December 14, 2017); pp. 50, 166 (*Spin*, March 16, 2011); p. 52 ("Noel Gallagher Rates Kanye West, Mustaches, and Ed Sheeran; Over/Under," posted November 27, 2017, by Pitchfork, YouTube); p. 62a (*NME*, December 10, 2005); p. 62b (*Music Feeds*, December 3, 2015); p. 62c (*Spin*, May 25, 2023); p. 62d (reprinted in *NME*, July 9, 2019); p. 62e (ShortList, October 16, 2011); p. 64 (reprinted in *NME*, November 14, 2012); p. 72 [bottom] (*The Guardian*, May 26, 2022); p. 80 [top] ("Oasis Interview—Noel Gallagher & Paul 'Bonehead' Arthurs [March 1995]," posted April 13, 2014, by TheRightEarOfNash, YouTube); pp. 86, 198 (*Vice*, August 9, 2017); p. 88 (*Exclaim!*, February 19, 2007); p. 94 ("I Can Still Muster Up That Rock 'n' Roll Temper": Liam Gallagher on His Triumphant Comeback," posted February 16, 2018, by *NME*, YouTube); p. 100 (*NME*, April 28, 2016); p. 102 ("10 Things Liam Loves/Hates," posted May 15, 2007, by timbuktukid, YouTube); p. 104 (October 22, 2011, Canal+ interview reprinted in *Daily Star*, October 23, 2011); p. 106 (NME, August 1, 2012); p. 108 [bottom] (February 14, 2011, BBC 6 Music interview reprinted in *Irish Independent*, February 18, 2011); p. 110 (MTV interview reprinted on Stop Crying Your Heart Out [fansite], November 15, 2011); p. 112 ("Oasis—'Definitely Maybe'—Noel Gallagher in Conversation with John Robb [Full Interview]," posted August 22, 2024, by oasisinetofficial, YouTube); p. 114 ("Liam Gallagher on Oasis Reunion & Love Island | Ask the Audience," posted June 9, 2002, by LADbible Entertainment, YouTube); p. 118a (*ShortList*, June 19, 2011); p. 118c (Digital Spy, March 20, 2010); p. 118d (*Mojo*, September 2011); p. 118e (2006 *NME* interview reprinted July 25, 2017); p. 120 [bottom] (*The Times* [London], October 8, 2009); p. 122 (*The Guardian*, June 15, 2002); p. 124 (StarWars.com, January 22, 2018); p. 140 ("Liam Gallagher vs. Cute Kids," posted February 20, 2018, by Noisey, YouTube); p. 146 (July 21, 2000, *Dotmusic* interview reprinted on sound.jp/oasis [fansite]); p. 148 [bottom] (Billboard.com, August 22, 2005); p. 150 [top] (*NME*, August 29, 2008); p. 158 (*GQ*, October 16, 2013); p. 160d (*NME*, July 10, 2015); p. 162 (*Rolling Stone*, May 2, 1996); p. 172 (*The Times*, July 18, 2010); p. 176 [top] ("Oasis Press Conference Stockholm 12 Sep 1997 Full Press Conference!," posted June 27, 2023, by Rolling Rockvideos, YouTube); p. 176 [bottom] (*The Irish Times*, May 27, 2023); p. 180 ("Noel Gallagher [Interview on The Jonathan Ross Show—2011-10-21]," posted October 23, 2011, by mrmonobrow67, YouTube); p. 182b (*CMJ New Music Monthly*, April 1996); p. 182d (@liamgallagher, X, April 11, 2024); p. 188a (*The Guardian*, August 15, 2012); p. 188b (Q, October 2016); p. 192 [top] (*NME*, June 2013); p. 194 (Q, March 2015); p. 196 (*Hot Press*, September 6, 1995); p. 204 (*Little White Lies*, October 3, 2016)

Redferns via Getty Images; p. 92 (top left) by Jon Super/Redferns via Getty Images; pp. 92 (top right), 121 by Kevin Mazur/One Love Manchester via Getty Images for One Love Manchester; p. 92 (bottom right) by Jana Legler/Redferns via Getty Images; p. 92 (bottom left) by Dave Simpson/WireImage via Getty Images; p. 93 (bottom right) by Ulrich Perrey/DPA Picture Alliance/Avalon; p. 93 (bottom left) by Jeff J. Mitchell via Getty Images; p. 97 by Splash News/Shutterstock; pp. 99, 127 by Backgrid/Shutterstock; p. 105 by Scott Heavey via Getty Images; p. 107 by Gary M. Prior via Getty Images; p. 119 (2) by Jesse Grant via Getty Images for Disney; p. 119 (3) by Benedict Johnson/Redferns via Getty Images; p. 119 (4) by Hirohisa Nakano/Contour by Getty Images; p. 119 (5) by Andy Willsher/Redferns via Getty Images; p. 125 by Richard Young/Shutterstock; p. 131 by Niki Nikolova/FilmMagic via Getty Images; p. 135 by Rebecca Naden, PA Images/PA Images via Getty Images; p. 137 by Gavin Smith/Camera Press London; p. 139 by Alan Clarke/Camera Press London; p. 143 by Rob Watkins/Alamy Stock Photo; p. 144 (top right) by Brian Rasic via Getty Images; p. 144 (bottom right) by Ricardo Rubio/Europa Press via Getty Images; p. 144 (bottom left) by Christina Radish/Redferns via Getty Images; p. 145 (top left) by Denis Jones/ANL/Shutterstock; p. 145 (top right) by Pete Still/Redferns via Getty Images; p. 145 (bottom right) by James Mccauley/Shutterstock; p. 145 (bottom left) by Roger Sargent/Shutterstock; pp. 146–147 by Mitchell Gerber/Corbis/VCG via Getty Images; p. 151 by United Plankton Pictures/Nickelodeon/Photo 12/Alamy Stock Photo; pp. 155, 161 (1) by JM International via Getty Images; p. 157 by Marcelo Hernandez via Getty Images; p. 159 by Dave J. Hogan via Getty Images; p. 161 (2) by Samir Hussein via Getty Images; p. 161 (4) by Anwar Hussein/Alamy Stock Photo; p. 161 (5) by Anthony Pidgeon/Redferns via Getty Images; pp. 164–165 by Danny Martindale/WireImage via Getty Images; p. 167 by David Abiaw/Shutterstock; pp. 168–169 by Sylvain Lefevre via Getty Images; p. 173 by David Dyson/Camera Press London; p. 175 by Matt Crossick/Alamy Stock Photo; p. 177 by Beretta/Sims/Shutterstock; p. 181 by David M. Benett via Getty Images for Facebook; p. 183 (1) by Dave M. Benett via Getty Images; p. 183 (5) by Francesco Guidicini/Camera Press London; p. 189 (1) by Ferdaus Shamim/WireImage via Getty Images; p. 189 (2) by Jim Dyson via Getty Images; p. 191 by Dave Thompson/Alamy Stock Photo; p. 193 by John Gunion/Redferns via Getty Images; p. 195 by Anton Corbijn/Contour by Getty Images; p 197 by Insidefoto/Alamy Stock Photo; pp. 198–199 by Oli Scarff/AFP via Getty Images.

Research: Parker Fishel and David Beal

Liam: It's nice to remind people that we're not just a bunch of silly old men calling each other "potato."

 **Liam Gallagher**
@liamgallagher

Potato

Simon & Schuster
1230 Avenue of the Americas
New York, NY 10020

First Simon & Schuster hardcover edition June 2025

SIMON & SCHUSTER and colophon are registered trademarks of Simon & Schuster, LLC

Simon & Schuster strongly believes in freedom of expression and stands against censorship in all its forms. For more information, visit BooksBelong.com.

For information about special discounts for bulk purchases, please contact Simon & Schuster Special Sales at 1-866-506-1949 or business@simonandschuster.com.

The Simon & Schuster Speakers Bureau can bring authors to your live event. For more information or to book an event, contact the Simon & Schuster Speakers Bureau at 1-866-248-3049 or visit our website at www.simonspeakers.com.

Interior design by Carly Loman

Manufactured in the United States of America

10 9 8 7 6 5 4 3 2 1

Library of Congress Cataloging-in-Publication Data is available.

ISBN 978-1-6682-0036-0
ISBN 978-1-6682-0038-4 (ebook)